MAR 1 1 2019

Rita Santos

MIKE
PENCE
US VICE PRESIDENT

E **Enslow Publishing**
101 W. 23rd Street
Suite 240
New York, NY 10011
USA
enslow.com

WORDS TO KNOW

activist A person who speaks out for a cause.

clinic A place that offers health services at low cost.

compromise An agreement where each side gives up something it wanted.

discriminate To treat someone unfairly.

evangelical A Christian who believes in being saved by following the word of the Bible.

immigrate To move from one country to another in order to live in that new country.

nominee A person who is chosen to run for a position.

protest A public demonstration to show disapproval of something.

veteran A person who was in the armed forces.

Contents

Mike Pence

CHAPTER 1

A FAMILY FULL OF FAITH

On June 7, 1959, Nancy and Edward Pence welcomed their newest son into the world. His name was Michael Richard Pence. Mike and his family grew up in Columbus, Indiana. Mike had three brothers and two sisters. His mother took care of the family. His father ran several gas stations. Edward Pence was also a **veteran** of the Korean War.

FAMILY ROOTS

As a child, Mike was close to his grandfather, Richard Michael Cawley. Mike loved to hear about how his grandfather had **immigrated** to the United States from

Mike's favorite ice cream flavor is moose tracks.

Irish immigrants arrive at Ellis Island.
Members of Mike's own family came
to America from Ireland.

Ireland. Richard had passed through Ellis Island on his
way to America. He joined his aunt and brother. They had
immigrated to Chicago a few years earlier. Like the rest
of his family, Mike was very proud of his Irish Catholic
background.

Life Choices

Mike finished high school in 1977. Next, he went to Hanover College in Hanover, Indiana. He studied history. While he was in college, Mike felt the need to serve his community. He had a hard time deciding how to do this. He was not sure if he wanted to be a Catholic priest or a politician. He wrestled with the choice for weeks.

Just for fun, Mike decided to join a group of friends on a weekend road trip. They attended a Christian music festival. There, Mike learned about **evangelical** Christianity. It changed his life. Mike became "born again." Mike said that he had found a more personal relationship with Jesus. He had been looking for this all of his life. He made up his mind. He would serve his community on the campaign trail.

Mike Pence Says:
"For me it all begins with faith."

Chapter 2
On the Radio!

While Pence was at law school, he met another evangelical Christian named Karen Whitaker. After separating from her first husband, Karen had become an elementary school teacher. Mike knew in his heart he was no longer Catholic. But he had not told his family yet. He and Karen were married in a Catholic ceremony in 1985. They would later have three children named Michael Jr., Charlotte, and Audrey. A few years after their wedding, Mike and Karen finally told his family he had changed his religion.

Pence the Politician

Pence ran for Congress twice but lost both times. During his second campaign, Pence chose to run negative ads. Many voters didn't like how he had behaved. After the race, Pence wrote an apology in the *Indiana Policy Review.*

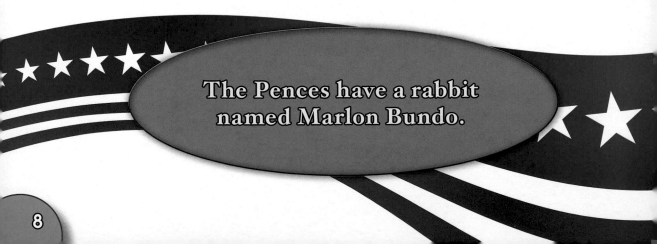

The Pences have a rabbit named Marlon Bundo.

Mike and his wife, Karen. The two met at church, where Karen played guitar.

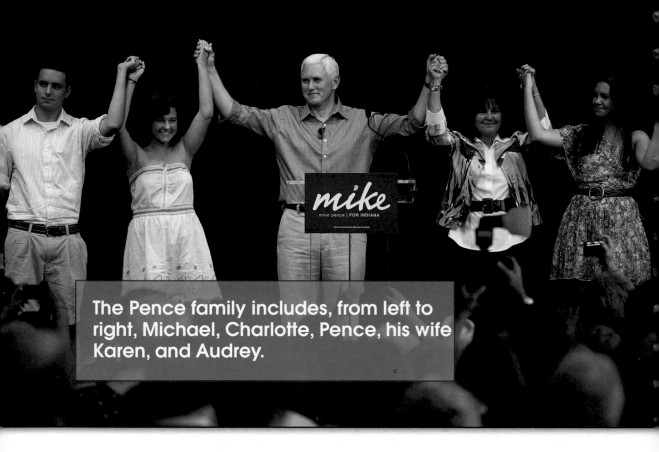

The Pence family includes, from left to right, Michael, Charlotte, Pence, his wife Karen, and Audrey.

He called it "Confessions of a Negative Campaigner." In the letter, he admitted he felt bad about the way he had run his campaign.

Mike Pence Says:
"I've always believed that civility in heavy doses is essential in self-government."

TALKING TO THE PEOPLE

In 1993, Pence decided to take a job hosting a radio show. It was called *The Mike Pence Show*. It aired on eighteen stations. On the show, he talked about his views on politics. People all over the state listened to him. He finally left the show to get back into politics. This time, in 2000, he was elected to the US House of Representatives.

Pence is surrounded by supporters during his 2000 campaign for the House of Representatives.

CHAPTER 3
IN THE GOVERNOR'S MANSION

Pence served four terms in the House of Representatives. He was known for listening to views even when he disagreed with them. Pence gained more power. Then, in 2012, he was voted the fiftieth governor of Indiana.

GETTING TO WORK

As governor, Pence was determined to cut taxes. He succeeded. With Pence as governor, Indiana saw the largest tax cut in the history of the state. He also helped the state's youngest students. Pence greatly increased the amount of money that was given to preschools.

Mike Pence Says:

"I'm a Christian, a conservative, and a Republican, in that order."

FAITH AT WORK

Pence is honest about what a big role his faith plays in his job. As governor, he defunded (took government money from) Planned Parenthoods in his state. This is a group that provides women's health services. Pence does not support them because some of their **clinics** give abortions. His faith states that abortions are wrong.

Pence speaks on the campaign trail in 2012 during his run for governor of Indiana.

Governor Pence greets the crowds at a county fair in Indiana in 2014.

THE RIGHTS OF THE PEOPLE

In 2015, Pence signed the Religious Freedom Restoration Act. It was meant to protect people's right to their religious beliefs. But the wording of it was unclear. Many were afraid that the bill could be used to discriminate

Governor Pence addresses Indiana lawmakers in 2013.

against the LGBTQ+ (lesbian, gay, bisexual, transgender, queer, and more) community. Thousands of people gathered in Indiana's largest cities to **protest** the bill. Pence decided to **compromise**. He changed the bill so that LGBTQ+ people would be protected from discrimination.

Pence's favorite movie is
The Wizard of Oz.

CHAPTER 4
ROAD TO THE WHITE HOUSE

In 2016, Donald Trump became the Republican **nominee** for president. He announced that Mike Pence would be his running mate. Being chosen to run for vice president of the United States was a great honor. But some of Pence's supporters wondered if it was a good idea to work with Trump.

AN UNLIKELY PAIR

Pence and Trump seemed to be total opposites in many ways. Trump was known for speaking his mind, and he often got himself into trouble. Pence had promised his voters that he would no longer use negative ads during his campaigns. But Trump ran many negative ads. Pence told his supporters that his running mate never pushed him to be negative. The two didn't always agree about everything. But they shared similar views for the country.

Mike Pence Says:

"Regardless of any title I'll ever hold, the most important job I'll ever have is spelled D-A-D."

Donald Trump gives Pence a thumbs-up at the Republican convention in 2016.

Pence discusses issues with Tim Kaine at a debate in 2016. Kaine was the Democratic nominee for vice president.

VICTORY

On November 8, 2016, Donald Trump was elected the forty-fifth American president. Mike Pence would be the vice president. On January 20, 2017, Mike Pence placed his hand over the Bible that he reads from every morning. He swore the oath of office of the vice president of the United States.

WORKING FOR THE PEOPLE

Pence got right to work in his new job. He attended many meetings and helped find people to fill positions in the new White House. He traveled to Asia and talked to world leaders. In late 2017, he made a surprise visit to Afghanistan. Pence met with American soldiers to show them his support. At home, he worked on passing a new tax bill through Congress.

Pence's time at the White House has not always been smooth sailing. His views on climate change, abortion,

Mike Pence is the sixth vice president from Indiana.

In 2018, Pence met with Benjamin Netanyahu, the prime minister of Israel. An important part of Pence's job as vice president is working with other world leaders.

human rights, and immigration have made him the target of many activists. But Pence continues to work hard and serve his country the best way he knows how.

TIMELINE

1959 Michael Richard Pence is born on June 7 in Columbus, Indiana.

1981 Earns a BA in History from Hanover College.

1985 Marries Karen Whitaker.

1986 Earns his law degree from Indiana University.

1988 Runs for Congress and loses.

1990 Runs for Congress for a second time. Loses again.

1991 Becomes president of the Indiana Policy Review Foundation.

1993 Begins hosting *The Mike Pence Show.*

2000 Is elected to the House of Representatives.

2012 Is elected governor of Indiana

2017 Becomes the vice president of the United States under President Donald Trump.

BOOKS

Mooney, Carla. *The U.S. Constitution: Discover How Democracy Works.* White River Jct., VT: Nomad Press, 2016.

Pence, Charlotte, and Karen Pence. *Marlon Bundo's Day in the Life of the Vice President.* Washington, DC: Regnery Kids, 2018.

Ransom, Candice. *What's Great About Indiana?* Minneapolis, MN: Lerner, 2015.

WEBSITES

Kiddle Mike Pence
kids.kiddle.co/Mike_Pence
Learn more about the life of Mike Pence.

Indiana
www.in.gov/core
Learn more about Mike's home state of Indiana.

Mike Pence
www.whitehouse.gov/people/mike-pence
Visit the official webpage of the vice president.

INDEX

Published in 2019 by Enslow Publishing, LLC.
101 W. 23rd Street, Suite 240, New York, NY 10011

Library of Congress Cataloging-in-Publication Data

Names: Santos, Rita, author.
Title: Mike Pence : US Vice President / Rita Santos.
Description: New York, NY : Enslow Publishing, 2019. | Series: Junior biographies | Includes bibliographical references and index. | Grades: 3-6. | Identifiers: LCCN 2018013649| ISBN 9781978502079 (library bound) | ISBN 9781978503038 (pbk.) | ISBN 9781978503045 (6 pack)
Subjects: LCSH: Pence, Mike, 1959- | Vice-Presidents—United States—Biography—Juvenile literature. | Governors—Indiana—Biography—Juvenile literature. | Legislators—United States—Biography—Juvenile literature. | Evangelicalism—Political aspects—United States—Juvenile literature. | Christian biography—United States—Juvenile literature. | United States—Politics and government—1989—Juvenile literature.
Classification: LCC E840.8.P376 S26 2019 | DDC 973.933092 [B] —dc23
LC record available at https://lccn.loc.gov/2018013649

Printed in the United States of America

To Our Readers: We have done our best to make sure all website addresses in this book were active and appropriate when we went to press. However, the author and the publisher have no control over and assume no liability for the material available on those websites or on any websites they may link to. Any comments or suggestions can be sent by email to customerservice@enslow.com.

Photos Credits: Cover, p. 1 Universal Images Group/Getty Images; pp. 2, 3, 22, 23, 24, back cover (curves graphic) Alena Kazlouskaya/Shutterstock.com; p. 4 Bloomberg/Getty Images; p. 6 Keystone-France/Gamma-Keystone/Getty Images; p. 9 Michael Hickey/Getty Images; pp. 10, 11, 13, 15 © AP Images; p. 14 Jeremy Hogan/Polaris/Newscom; p. 18 Timothy A. Clary/AFP/Getty Images; p. 19 Saul Loeb/AFP/Getty Images; p. 21 Ariel Schalit/AFP/Getty Images; interior page bottoms (stars and stripes) Razym/Shutterstock.com.